# This book belongs to:

.......................................................

# Notes for Parents

- Encourage your child to find the picture stickers and answer the questions in the book.

- Use the gold star stickers to praise their successes, and to encourage their sensible money habits.

- Fill in the 'I will' tasks on the wipe-clean reward chart, and the star targets and rewards. Your child will enjoy joining in with this too, particularly in choosing the rewards. They will love the sense of responsibility, and the excitement of working towards the treats they've chosen.

- Rewards need not be big, but they should be meaningful to your child: an extra bedtime story, baking a cake together, going to the swimming pool or the park, having a friend to play – something that they enjoy, and that you feel is appropriate to what they have achieved.

- Always keep a positive attitude and remember to focus on their achievements. Never take away stickers or deny a reward that has been agreed and earned.

- Your child will appreciate that having good money sense can be fun, and these positive early habits will help to encourage them to grow to be responsible and thoughtful people.

ISBN 978-1-78270-065-4

Copyright © 2014 Award Publications Limited

First published 2014

Published by Award Publications Limited,
The Old Riding School, The Welbeck Estate,
Worksop, Nottinghamshire, S80 3LR

16 3

Printed in Turkey

# The Children's Book of
# MONEY
# SENSE

Sophie Giles

Illustrated by Kate Davies

AWARD PUBLICATIONS LIMITED

Darius really wants a new video game that is coming out soon. His parents give him pocket money, but he spends it on sweets and comics. When the game is released he hasn't enough money left to buy it.

**Why can't Darius afford to buy the game?**

Darius decides to stop wasting his money and works hard to earn more by doing extra chores at home. He is so excited to be able to go and buy the game with the money that he has saved.

I save up for things I want

**Do you save your money?**

Ellie has lost her money for the school cake sale. Instead of keeping it safe inside a purse, she put the money in her pocket

and it fell out when she was playing football. Without her money she can't buy a cake.

**Why is Ellie upset?**

When Ellie needs to take money to school, she keeps it safely in a purse with her name inside. She understands how important it is to keep money in a safe place, and what can happen if she doesn't.
**Do you look after your money?**

I keep my money safe

Last year, Zac used up all his spending money on the first day of his holiday. Later in the week, when he saw a new toy that

he wanted, he couldn't afford to buy it. Zac's older sister tells him he should have budgeted more carefully.

**Why can't Zac buy the toy?**

This year, Zac knows how much he has to spend, and is careful to make it last so that he still has some money left on the very last day of the holiday. This is called budgeting your money.

I can budget my money

**Do you budget your money?**

Emily loves the new game on her tablet. But by buying extra items in the game without asking her mum's permission she has run up an enormous bill. Emily's mum is very cross that she has spent a lot of money.

**Why is Emily in trouble?**

Emily knows now that it can be very easy to spend money in games and online without realising. She always asks her mum to check and help her if she wants to buy items in games or on the internet.
**Do you ask before spending online in games?**

I ask permission before I buy items in games

Ruby and Robbie's dad is upset because their latest electricity bill is very high. The family look around the house and find

many lights and appliances switched on but not being used. This is wasting money.

**What has caused the big bill?**

The family's electricity bills are much lower now that everyone turns off lights when they are not needed. And instead of leaving appliances on standby, they turn them off completely.

**Do you help make savings at home and at school?**

I help make savings

Declan and his older brother, Oscar, have been to the cinema. Oscar paid for their tickets, sweets and popcorn using his debit

card. When he tries to take cash out of the ATM for their bus fare home, there is no money left in his account. **Why is there no money?**

Dad explains that Oscar's cash card takes money straight out of his savings account. Now Oscar understands that spending using a card is just the same as handing over banknotes and coins.

**Do you understand how your money works?**

I know how money works

The children would like some new playground equipment at school, but the the head teacher explains that there isn't enough money to buy any at the moment. The children are disappointed.

**Why can't the school buy new playground equipment?**

With the help of their teachers and parents, the children hold a fundraising day, with all sorts of stalls and fun games. Soon they have raised enough money to buy new playground equipment!
**How could you help to raise money?**

Gemma is showing off her new trainers.
She tells the other children how expensive
they were, and laughs at Luke because
his trainers are old and worn.
Luke runs home in tears.

**What did Gemma do
to make Luke cry?**

Dan explains that Luke's dad has just lost his job, so the family don't have money for new trainers. Gemma apologises to Luke and learns to be more sensitive to other people's circumstances.

**Are you understanding about other people's situations?**

I consider the feelings of others

Ollie has saved half of his pocket money every week for a whole year, and is really pleased to have saved so much! But sadly the family's house is burgled, and the thief steals all of Ollie's savings too.

**Where did Ollie keep all of his savings?**

Ollie's grandad takes him to open up his very own bank account. Ollie now puts most of his savings in the bank where they will be safe. He even earns a little extra money from the bank too, called 'interest'!

**Do you have a savings account?**

SAVINGS BANK

I have a savings account

It is pocket-money day and Sheena wants to go to bowling with her friends, but she can't afford to because she must pay back  the money her brother loaned her last week to buy a t-shirt that she wanted.

**Why is Sheena giving her brother her pocket money?**

Sheena realises that it is better to save up for what she wants than to borrow money. Next time she receives her pocket money, it is all hers, to spend or save as she pleases.

**Are you sensible with your pocket money?**

I think before I borrow money

Will asks if he can ride Ted's new bike. When Will's mum calls them both in for dinner, Will carelessly drops the bike on the ground, smashing the light. Ted is upset that Will has damaged his new bike.

**Why is Ted sad?**

Will's mum tells him he must save up his pocket money to replace Ted's bike light. Will learns to respect other people's belongings, and realises that some things are not always replaced so easily.

I respect other people's property

**Do you respect others' things?**

It is Friday night and Nathan and his family are about to order a takeaway pizza as a treat. On the television in the background

is an advert for a charity appealing for donations to help homeless people.
**Who does the charity want to help with their donations?**

It is cold outside and Nathan and his sister are thankful to have a warm house to live in. They ask if they can make pizza at home and donate the money they save to the charity for the homeless.

I donate to charity

**Do you donate to charity?**

Amy spends all of her pocket money on a magazine with a free packet of sweets. Soon all the sweets are eaten and Amy

is bored with the magazine. Mum asks Amy if she thinks it was good value for money. **Why was the magazine not very good value?**

The next week, Amy spots a book at the supermarket that she would like to read. It is the same price as the magazine she bought, and will last much longer! Amy tells Mum that it is very good value.

I know good value for money

**Do you know good value?**

# Money Around the World

Throughout history, many things have been used as money: camels, barley, clam shells – all sorts of things! Eventually, money as we know it today (notes and metal coins) became the favoured way to buy and sell things. It's much easier to carry in your purse or wallet than ten camels!

Did you know that money is different all around the world? This means the notes and coins that you use in your country are not necessarily the same as those used in other places.

The money a country uses is called its *currency*. There are over 180 currencies in the world. Different currencies have their own symbols, and the notes and coins look different too!

If you go on holiday abroad you might need to change your spending money into the currency of the country that you are visiting. You can do this at a *bureau de change*.

# Bureau de Change

When you change your money, it is done according to an *exchange rate*. This means that at the moment of changing, your money is worth a certain amount of the new currency.

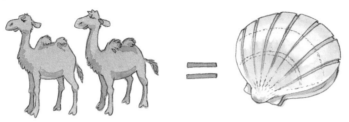

For example, if the exchange rate is two camels to one clam shell, and you have one clam shell to change, you will receive two camels. And if you had 100 clam shells, you would receive 200 camels. What a lot of camels that would be!

## Help Zig Exchange His Money

Zig the alien is visiting Earth on holiday. On the planet Zag where he comes from, the currency is 'zonks'. Using the table below can you help Zig to figure out what his 10 Zonk banknote will be exchanged for in the following currencies?

| Currency | Exchange Rate | 10 Zonks Equals... |
|----------|---------------|--------------------|
| British pounds | 1 zonk = £2.00 | £ _____ |
| US dollars | 1 zonk = $1.50 | $ _____ |
| Euros | 1 zonk = €0.50 | € _____ |
| Nigerian naira | 1 zonk = ₦10.00 | ₦ _____ |
| Chinese yuan | 1 zonk = ¥4.00 | ¥ _____ |
| Singapore dollars | 1 zonk = S$3.50 | S$ _____ |

Turn the page to check your answers!

# Important Words

 To **owe** someone means you have borrowed something, usually money, and need to pay it back.

A **donation** is a gift given to help someone in need. It is often money, but it can also be other things, such as food or clothes.

 To **earn** money people need to work in a job. The money they earn is called a **wage** or a **salary**.

**Interest** is money that the bank adds to your savings. The more money you have in your account, the more interest that money will earn.

 A **budget** is a plan of how to save and spend your money.

**Fundraising** is when an event is held to raise money for a charity or cause.

Answers: Zig will receive £20, $15, €3, ₦100, ¥40, S$35

Encourage your child to use the picture stickers and answer the questions in the book.

I think before I borrow money

I keep my money safe

I save up for things I want

I ask permission before I buy items in games

I have a savings account

I know how money works

I help make savings

I can budget my money

I help to raise money

I donate to charity

I respect other people's property

I consider the feelings of others

I know good value for money

Use these gold star stickers to praise your child's successes and encourage their progress.